Greeting Customers on the Lot

How to Approach Buyers Without Pressure

Bruce Huddleston

Bedrock Heritage Publishing

Published by Bedrock Heritage Publishing

A Division of Life Guidance Consulting LLC

Tyler, Texas

www.bedrockheritagepublishing.com

ISBN: 978-1-972179-13-0 (Paperback)

ISBN: 978-1-972179-66-6 EPUB)

Manufactured in the United States of America

DISCLAIMER

This book is based on the author's personal and professional experiences, observations, and opinions accumulated over a thirty-five year career in the automotive industry. It is intended for educational and informational purposes only.

The stories and anecdotes contained in this book are drawn from real-world situations encountered throughout the author's career. However, names, identifying details, specific circumstances, employer names, dealership names, and individual characteristics have been changed, omitted, combined, or fictionalized to protect the privacy of the individuals involved. Any resemblance to specific living persons, current or former employers, or existing businesses is coincidental and unintentional.

No individual, dealership, organization, or employer referenced or implied in the stories within this book has reviewed, approved, or endorsed the content herein. The recollections and characterizations presented are solely the author's own perspective and memory of events and do not constitute a factual record, legal testimony, or statement of fact regarding any identifiable person or entity.

The sales strategies, techniques, and professional advice presented in this book reflect the author's personal approach and experience. Individual results will vary based on experience, effort, market conditions, dealership policies, and other factors beyond the author's control. Nothing in this book constitutes a guarantee of income, employment, or professional outcome.

For every salesperson who ever walked out that door
not sure what to say.
You already have what it takes.
This book is about learning to use it.

FREE BONUS

Your Complete Digital Script Library

Get the Car Sales Survival Quick-Reference Card — a free companion to this book that puts the key rules and techniques on one page you can keep at your desk.

Visit:

www.carsalessurvivalseries.com/scripts

Enter your email to claim your free reader bonus.

Print it. Keep it. Use it.

Contents

INTRODUCTION

The Approach Is the Sale

Most salespeople think the sale starts when the customer says yes. It doesn't.

It starts when you walk out that door.

Everything you do between the moment that car pulls in and the moment you say your first word sets the tone for everything that follows. The pace you walk. Where you position yourself. Whether you make eye contact too soon or not soon enough. Whether you look like someone going to greet a person or someone going to close a deal.

Customers read all of it. They read it fast, and they read it accurately.

I've watched salespeople lose deals before they opened their mouths. I've watched them sprint across a lot, stick out a hand, and start talking—and I already knew before they got there that the customer was going to leave. Because the customer knew too, they saw the approach, and the approach told them everything they needed to know.

Here's the thing: most training doesn't tell you that customers arrive defensive. Not because they're bad people. Because every instinct they've developed about car lots tells them to be. They've heard the stories. Some of them have lived the stories. They pull into that lot expecting someone to come at them, and the moment you confirm that expectation, you've already lost ground you may not get back.

The approach is your first opportunity to be different. To be the person who doesn't fit the stereotype they walked in with.

That's what this book is about.

We're not going to talk about closing techniques or objection handling. That comes later. This book is about the moment before any of that—the walk across the lot, the read you do before you arrive, the words you choose first, and how you handle it when things don't go the way you planned.

Get the approach right, and everything that follows gets easier. Get it wrong, and you spend the rest of the conversation fighting to recover ground you gave away in the first ten seconds.

One skill at a time. This is the one that starts everything.

"The Rule: The sale doesn't start when the customer says yes. It starts the moment they see you coming."

CHAPTER I

WHY THE APPROACH MAKES OR BREAKS THE DEAL

THE APPROACH IS THE most misunderstood moment in car sales.

Most salespeople treat it like a formality—something to get through on the way to the real conversation. Walk out, say hello, ask what they're looking for. Simple. Routine. No big deal.

It's a very big deal.

Here's why. When a customer pulls onto your lot, they don't know you yet. They don't know if you're going to be helpful or pushy, honest or slick, someone they can trust or someone they need to protect themselves from. All they have to go on is what they see. And what they see, in those first few seconds, is the approach.

That approach answers every silent question they walked in with.

Is this going to be comfortable or uncomfortable? Is this person going to help me or work me? Can I take my time here, or will someone be on top of me the second I step out of the car?

You answer those questions whether you mean to or not. The only question is whether you answer them in your favor.

What the Research Won't Tell You

You can read about psychological studies on personal space and threat response. You can learn that humans make trust assessments in milliseconds. That's all true, and none of it will help you as much as thirty seconds of observation before you walk out the door.

I'm not interested in theory. I'm interested in what actually happens on the lot. And what actually happens is this: the customers who feel comfortable stay. The customers who feel pressured leave. And the difference, more often than not, comes down to the approach.

I've seen salespeople with better product knowledge, better closing skills, and better track records than their colleagues lose deal after deal because their approach triggered every alarm the customer walked in with. And I've seen average salespeople with average skills sell cars consistently because they learned how to walk across a lot without making a customer feel hunted.

The approach is a skill. It's learnable. And it's worth learning before you develop habits that are hard to break.

The Cost of Getting It Wrong

When the approach goes wrong, you usually don't know it right away. The customer doesn't say, "Your approach made me uncomfortable, so I'm leaving." They say, "I'm just looking." Or they give you ten minutes of short answers before they drift back to their car. Or they leave entirely.

You chalk it up to a bad up. Not a serious buyer. Wrong time.

Sometimes that's true. But sometimes—more often than most salespeople want to admit—you made that decision for them. Not with anything you said. With how you came at them.

Every customer you lose in the first 60 seconds is a deal that never gets a chance. You don't get to show them the inventory. You don't get to find out what they actually need. You don't get to demonstrate anything. They're already gone, and all you have left is a story about how they were just looking.

The Cost of Getting It Right

When the approach is right, the whole conversation changes.

The customer relaxes. Their guard comes down—not completely, not right away, but enough. They start talking. They tell you things they came in planning to keep to themselves, because you didn't come at them like someone they needed to protect themselves from.

That's when the real conversation can happen.

Getting the approach right doesn't guarantee a sale. Nothing guarantees a sale. But it gives you a fighting chance. It gets you into the conversation, and a lot of good things can happen there.

That's the goal of this book—not to hand you a script, but to help you understand what you're doing on that walk across the lot and why it matters. When you understand it, you can adjust it. When you can adjust it, you can get consistently better results.

Start there. Everything else follows.

"The Rule: A bad approach doesn't just cost you a greeting. It costs you the conversation—and everything that conversation could have led to."

CHAPTER 2

WHAT CUSTOMERS ARE THINKING BEFORE YOU REACH THEM

B Y THE TIME YOU reach that customer, they've already had a conversation. You weren't part of it.

It happened in the car on the way over, at dinner last night, or in the quiet moment before they pulled in. They talked about what they want and what they don't want. What they can spend and what they don't want to admit they can spend. Whether they're here to buy or here to look. Whether they're going to tell the salesperson any of that.

They've also, to some degree, decided what the salesperson will be like. Most of them aren't expecting a great experience. They're expecting someone who's going to push, ask too many questions too fast, and make this harder than it needs to be.

That's the room you're walking into before you say a word.

The Defense Mechanism

There's a reason customers cross their arms when a salesperson approaches. There's a reason they say "I'm just looking" before you've asked them anything. They're not being difficult. They're protecting themselves from an experience they've either had before or heard about from someone who has.

The defense mechanism kicks in the moment they see you coming. They start calculating. How fast is he walking? Is he going to try to steer me somewhere immediately? Is she going to ask me what my budget is before I've even looked at anything?

Every move you make either confirms their fears or starts to dissolve them. That's the dynamic you're working inside.

You can't eliminate the defense mechanism. What you can do is choose not to trigger it. A calm pace, an open posture, a greeting that doesn't demand anything from them immediately—these are the things that start to lower the wall. Not all at once. But enough to have a conversation.

What They Actually Want

Here's what most customers actually want, even if they'd never say it out loud.

They want to feel like they're in control of the process. They want to look at what they want to look at, at the pace they want to look at it, without someone directing them somewhere they didn't choose to go.

They want to be treated like an adult who is capable of making a large purchase without being managed.

They want information when they ask for it, help when they need it, and space in between.

And underneath all of that, even the most guarded customer wants this to go well. They're here because they want a car. That desire is already working for you. Your job is not to get in the way of it.

The Salesperson They're Hoping For

Most customers walk in expecting a bad experience and hoping for a good one. They're hoping for someone who listens. Someone who doesn't make them feel stupid for not knowing exactly what they want. Someone who gives them information without an agenda attached to every sentence.

They're hoping for someone who makes this easier than they thought it would be.

That's not a high bar. But you have to get through the approach first before any of that becomes possible.

FROM THE FLOOR

I was sitting in the front lobby of a dealership I managed—glass-fronted, with a full view of the lot. A car pulled in. Two salespeople inside saw it at the same time. They both jumped up, ran for the door, and literally shoved each other, trying to get through it first, pushing and shoving like it was a race.

The customers, still in their car, watched every second of this.

The winner was out of breath when he got there. He stuck his hand out and started talking before he'd even caught his breath, never looked at the wife, never acknowledged the kids in the back seat. Just started in.

The family looked around for a few minutes and left.

When I asked what happened, the salesperson said: "They were just looking."

No. They were watching. And what they watched told them everything they needed to know about what the next hour would feel like. The sprint didn't just cost a deal; it cost a deal. It answered every one of the customer's silent questions about this place—and none of the answers were good.

That story lives in my head every time I talk about the approach. Because it illustrates exactly what I mean when I say customers are watching before you reach them.

They pulled in as potential buyers. They left as people who'd already made a decision—and that decision happened before anyone said hello.

What are customers thinking before you reach them? They're thinking about whether this is going to be what they feared. Give them a reason to think otherwise.

"The Rule: Customers decide how this is going to feel before you open your mouth. The approach is your only chance to change the answer they've already started forming."

CHAPTER 3

THE RIGHT DISTANCE: HOW CLOSE IS TOO CLOSE

NOBODY TALKS ABOUT DISTANCE. It's one of the most practical things about the approach, and most sales training skips right past it.

How close you get, how fast you close that distance, and where you position yourself when you arrive—all of it sends a signal. And customers read that signal before they hear a single word.

The Problem with Getting Too Close Too Fast

When you walk directly up to a customer and get within two or three feet immediately, you've entered their personal space before they've had a chance to decide whether they're comfortable with it. For most people, that's a threat response. Not a dramatic one. But it's there.

The body reacts to proximity the way it reacts to pressure. Shoulders come up. Arms cross. The person takes a step back—literally or figuratively. They go into protection mode.

You didn't do anything wrong yet. You didn't say anything wrong. But the physical approach itself put them on the defensive, and now you're starting the conversation from behind.

This is more common than you'd think. Salespeople who are eager, friendly, and extroverted—they naturally close the distance fast. It's how they operate with people they know. On the lot, with a stranger who didn't invite the interaction, it reads differently.

The Problem with Hanging Back

On the other end of it, if you hang back and approach from too far away—or worse, if you call out a greeting from twenty feet—you're either going to seem lazy or make the customer feel like they have to project their voice to have a conversation.

Neither is what you want. The greeting needs to feel personal. It can't feel personal if you're shouting across the lot.

The Right Distance

Aim for six to eight feet when you arrive. That's close enough to be clearly engaged—this is a real conversation, not a wave from across the lot—and far enough that you're not in their space before they've had a chance to get comfortable.

From that distance, you introduce yourself, make eye contact, and let them set the next move. If they step toward you, that's an invitation to close the gap. If they stay where they are, stay where you are.

Match their cues. Don't close distance because you're comfortable with proximity. Close it because they've indicated they're comfortable with it.

Where You Position Yourself

Position matters too. Standing directly in front of someone—squarely facing them—is more confrontational than it feels from your side. It's face-to-face, which is how people stand when they're about to argue.

A slight angle is better. Forty-five degrees or so. It's less direct, less confrontational, and it creates a sense of side-by-side rather than face-off. Subtly, it positions you as someone who's with them—not across from them.

If they're looking at a vehicle, try to approach it from the side rather than from between them and the vehicle. Don't block what they're trying to see. Let them keep looking. You're arriving alongside the moment, not interrupting it.

Movement Speed

Walk at a normal pace. Not slow—that looks like you're reluctant. Not fast—that looks like you're coming at them.

Normal. The pace you'd walk toward a neighbor you wanted to say hello to. Relaxed, deliberate, friendly.

That pace communicates something. It says: I'm coming over to help, not because I'm racing to claim this customer before someone else does. Customers can feel the difference.

Distance is a tool. Use it like one.

"The Rule: The distance you keep when you arrive tells the customer whether you're coming to help them or coming at them. Get it right before you say hello."

CHAPTER 4

READING THE CUSTOMER BEFORE YOU ARRIVE

BEFORE YOU TAKE A step toward that customer, you have a few seconds to watch. Use them.

That brief window—between when they pull in and when you go out—gives you information you can't get any other way. It tells you what kind of customer you're dealing with, what they may already have in mind, and how you should approach them.

Most salespeople skip this step. They see a customer, they go. That's a missed opportunity every time.

What to Watch For

First, watch where they go.

A customer who steps out of their car and walks directly toward a specific vehicle already knows something. They've done research. They have a model in mind, a type they're looking for, or something they saw online and came to look at in person. That's a different conversation from the one with the customer who wanders.

The wanderer is still exploring. They may know their general parameters—something bigger, something more fuel efficient, something newer—but they don't have a target yet. They need space and time before they're ready to talk specifics.

Watch where they walk. It tells you how far along they are.

Read the Body Language

Posture tells you a lot about comfort level.

A customer who gets out of the car, stretches, looks around with an open expression—relaxed shoulders, moving at an easy pace—is generally in a comfortable state of mind. They're open. Not necessarily ready to buy, but not defensive either.

A customer who gets out of the car and immediately starts looking around—scanning the lot, or looking for exits, or moving quickly to put a vehicle between themselves and the entrance—is in a more guarded state. They came prepared to manage the experience. They're going to need a lighter touch.

Crossed arms, tight posture, short movements—all of these signal someone who needs more space before they're comfortable. Give it to them. You'll get more out of the conversation if you let them settle.

Who's in the Car

Notice who came with them.

A solo buyer is a different conversation than a couple. A couple with kids is different again. The number of people who got out of that car changes how you approach and who you make eye contact with first.

We'll go deeper on this in the chapters on specific customer types. For now, the point is simple: notice who's there before you arrive, so you're not improvising when you get there.

If it's a couple, don't ignore the passenger. That's a deal-killer that's been around as long as car sales have, and it's still happening on lots everywhere. The passenger is part of the decision. Sometimes the passenger is the one who makes most of the decisions.

What They're Driving

Take a quick look at what they pulled up in. It's not a profile, and you're not going to make assumptions about what they can afford based on their current vehicle. Don't do that. It's a bad habit that costs deals.

But what they're driving can tell you something about what they're used to. A pickup truck driver looking at your truck inventory is probably comfortable with that category. A sedan driver who walks to the SUV section is probably making a lifestyle change. That context helps you ask better questions.

The Pause Before the Walk

This whole read takes about 10 to 15 seconds. That's not long. But it's the difference between walking out cold and walking out with a head start.

You know roughly where they are mentally. You know who you're approaching. You know what they've already gravitated toward. You're not guessing when you get there—you're working with something.

Those ten seconds of observation are one of the most underused tools in the lot approach. Most salespeople are already in motion. Slow it down. Watch first. Then walk.

"The Rule: Read before you walk. The few seconds between them pulling in and you going out are the only free information you'll get about who they are and what they need."

Chapter 5

The Words That Open — and the Words That Close

Most salespeople spend a lot of time thinking about what to say when they greet a customer. They want the perfect line. The opener that disarms, connects, and sets the whole conversation in motion.

Here's the truth: the words matter less than you think. And a few specific words matter more than you realize.

What you're really choosing when you choose your opening line is whether you're asking something of the customer or offering something to them. That's the distinction that matters. And most salespeople, without realizing it, open by asking.

The Words That Close

Some opening lines are so common they've become invisible. Salespeople say them automatically. Customers hear them and immediately put up their guard—also automatically.

"Can I help you find something today?"

That's a yes-or-no question. And the answer, nine times out of ten, is no. Not because the customer doesn't want help. Because they're not ready to say yes to anything yet. You just handed them an exit, and they took it.

"What brings you in today?"

Better than the first one, but it still demands information before you've earned it. The customer just got here. They haven't decided whether they trust you yet. Asking them to explain their situation in the first ten seconds puts them on the spot.

"Are you looking to buy today?"

This one's almost aggressive. You're asking them to commit to an intention before they've looked at a single vehicle. Most customers will say no just to protect their options—even if they came in ready to buy.

These lines close the conversation down. Not all the way. But they create resistance before you've had a chance to create comfort. You spend the next five minutes trying to open a door you just nudged shut.

The Words That Open

Simple is better. Pressure-free is better. A greeting that asks nothing of the customer in the first moment—that gives them something without requiring anything back—is the opening that works.

"Good afternoon. I'm Bruce—welcome in."

That's it: a greeting, a name, a welcome. No question. No ask. No demand. The customer received something—a name, a friendly acknowledgment—without being asked to give anything in return. That changes the dynamic.

"Take your time looking around. I'll be right here if anything comes up."

This one explicitly permits them to be where they are. You're not pushing them toward a conversation. You're telling them the conversation is available when they want it. That's a completely different message than anything that starts with "Can I help you?"

"Hey—glad you came in. Let me know if you have any questions."

Casual, genuine, low-pressure. It lands as friendly rather than transactional. The customer doesn't feel like a lead. They feel like a person who walked in somewhere and got a normal human greeting.

What Comes After

The opening line isn't designed to start a conversation. It's designed to make the customer comfortable enough that they'll start one when they're ready.

Sometimes that's immediately. They respond to your greeting and keep talking. Great—follow their lead.

Sometimes they nod and return to looking at the vehicle ahead of them. Also great. You've introduced yourself, made it clear you're available, and haven't made them feel cornered. Stay nearby. Let them come to the next moment.

The mistake most salespeople make is treating the opening line like it has to accomplish everything. It doesn't. Its only job is to make the next moment possible. Keep it simple enough to do that job and nothing more.

Tone Is Half the Message

Whatever words you use, tone carries half the weight. A warm opening delivered in a flat, mechanical voice reads as a script. A simple greeting delivered with genuine ease reads as a real person.

Customers know the difference. They've heard the scripts. What they respond to—what actually lowers the guard—is the sense that there's a real person on the other side of the interaction. Not someone performing friendliness. Someone who actually is.

You can't fake that long-term. But you can be aware of it in the moment. When you walk out to greet a customer, be a person first. The salesperson part can come once they know who they're talking to.

"The Rule: Your opening line has one job: make the next moment possible. Keep it simple, keep it genuine, and ask nothing of the customer before they're ready to give it."

CHAPTER 6

APPROACHING THE SOLO BUYER

THE SOLO BUYER IS, in some ways, the most straightforward customer you'll approach. There's no group dynamic to navigate, no second person whose comfort level you're monitoring, no conversation happening between them that you have to wait for a break in.

It's just the two of you.

That simplicity is also its own kind of pressure. With a couple or a group, if one person goes quiet, another might keep things moving. With a solo buyer, if the conversation stalls, you're both left standing there. The stakes of the approach feel higher because there's no one else to absorb the awkward.

Understanding who the solo buyer usually is helps you approach them more effectively.

Who Comes Alone

Solo buyers generally fall into a few categories.

The decisive buyer came alone on purpose. They already know what they want—or at least which category they're shopping in—and they didn't bring anyone because they don't need anyone else's opinion. They're efficient. They want information, not conversation. Match their pace.

The private buyer doesn't want anyone in their business. Maybe it's a financial situation they're navigating on their own. Maybe they just prefer to make decisions without input. They came alone because this is private. Give them space and let them open up on their own terms.

The early-stage researcher is just gathering information before they involve anyone else. They're not ready to decide. They want to look without pressure, form an opinion, and then maybe bring someone back. They're not a weak lead—they're a methodical one.

You usually can't tell which one you're dealing with from across the lot. The read you did before you walked out helps. But the approach itself should work for all three.

The Approach

With a solo buyer, give yourself slightly more distance than you might with a couple. When it's one person, your presence is more concentrated. There's no one else to look at, nowhere else to direct their attention. You're it—six to eight feet, a relaxed pace, and an opening that doesn't box them in.

Make genuine eye contact. Not a stare—a normal, friendly acknowledgment. Then introduce yourself and give them the out.

"Hey there—I'm Bruce. Take your time looking around, and let me know if anything comes up."

Simple. Low-key. You've introduced yourself and made clear you're available without attaching yourself to them.

Reading the Response

After that opener, watch what they do.

If they engage—if they respond to the greeting with more than a nod, if they ask a question, if they start telling you something—they're inviting you in. Step into that. Match their energy, ask a follow-up question, and start building the conversation.

If they give you a short response and turn back to what they were looking at, they're not ready yet. Don't push. Stay in range, stay available, and let them come to the next moment.

The solo buyer who needs a little time to warm up is not a lost cause. They're a person who processes before they engage. Give them something to process—the vehicles on the lot, a little bit of space—and check back naturally in a few minutes.

"Have you had a chance to look inside that one yet? I can grab the keys if you want to sit in it."

That's a light, practical offer. It's not a push. It's a door.

The Conversation That Builds

Once the solo buyer starts talking, the conversation tends to move faster than it would with a group. There's no one to defer to, no one to check with before answering. It's direct.

Use that. Ask good questions. Listen to what they actually say, not just to what you expected them to say. Solo buyers who feel genuinely heard tend to open up more than you might expect from someone who came in guarded.

The person who walked in alone and quiet is often the same person who, twenty minutes later, is telling you exactly what they need and why they need it—because you gave them the space to get there.

FROM THE FLOOR

The summer heat in Texas is no joke. I was managing a used-car lot—no air conditioning on the lot, obviously—and it was one of those July afternoons when the asphalt is soft, and the air feels like a wet towel. A couple pulled in. I watched my newest salesperson sprint out to meet them—which was already the wrong move—and by the time he got to them he was visibly sweating through his shirt. The customers looked at him, looked at each other, and said they were just looking. He came back inside looking defeated.

I went out. Introduced myself. Said: "Sorry about the heat—let me know if you want to step inside and cool off while we talk." That's all it took. They came inside. We sold them a car in ninety minutes. The first salesperson did everything wrong before he said a word. I did one thing right: I acknowledged where they were before I asked anything of them.

That story is about a couple, but the principle applies to every solo buyer as well. Acknowledge where they are. Not just physically—emotionally. Meet them at their comfort level, not yours. That's the approach that gets the conversation started.

"The Rule: With a solo buyer, your presence is concentrated. Give them a little more space, a little more time, and a door they can walk through when they're ready."

Chapter 7

Approaching Couples and Groups

When more than one person gets out of that car, the approach gets more complicated. Not harder—just more layered. There are multiple people in front of you, each with their own comfort level, their own investment in the decision, and their own read on whether this will be a good experience.

Your job is to make all of them feel included. The moment you focus entirely on one person and let the other become a spectator, you've started losing ground.

The Mistake That Kills More Deals Than Any Other

You already know what it is. Every sales trainer who's ever stood in front of a room of car salespeople has said it. And it's still happening on lots everywhere, every day.

Ignoring the passenger.

It's almost always the driver who gets the greeting. Eye contact goes to the driver. The handshake goes to the driver. The questions go to the driver. The passenger—whoever they are, whatever role they're playing in this decision—gets a nod if they're lucky.

Here's the problem. In a significant percentage of couples' purchases, the passenger is the decision-maker. Or co-decision-maker. Or the person who has veto power. You don't know which is going in. And if you've spent the first ten minutes of the conversation talking exclusively to one person while the other stands there feeling invisible, you've made an enemy out of someone who had no reason to be one.

Acknowledge both people. From the first moment. Eye contact with both. Use both names as soon as you learn them.

The Opening With a Couple

Approach as you would with any customer—calmly, at an appropriate distance, with an open posture. When you get there, make eye contact with both people as you introduce yourself. Not a quick glance at one and then a long look at the other. A genuine acknowledgment of both.

"Hey—I'm Bruce. Welcome in. Take your time looking around, and let me know if you have any questions."

Said while making eye contact with both of them. Not alternating robotically—naturally, the way you would if you were talking to two people you already knew.

From there, let the conversation develop. One of them will typically take the lead in responding. Fine—engage with them. But don't let the other disappear. Circle back. Ask them directly. Make sure they know you're talking to both of them.

When One Person Is Clearly the Driver

Sometimes one person is obviously more engaged than the other. They're the ones asking questions, looking at stickers, opening doors. The other person is following along, looking at their phone, holding the kids' hands.

It's tempting to let the engaged person carry the conversation and treat the other as secondary. Don't.

The quiet one is still part of this decision. They may be less interested in the details and more interested in the overall feel—whether this place seems trustworthy, whether this salesperson seems honest, whether they'd be comfortable here for the next couple of hours.

Those are not small things. Those are often the things that determine whether the deal happens.

Find natural moments to include them. Ask a question that's genuinely directed at them. Not forced—natural. "Is this going to be for both of you, or mainly for one?" "Are there any features that are important to you specifically?" Let them contribute. They may not have much to say, but the fact that you asked matters.

Groups with Kids

Kids on the lot change the dynamic. The parents are now managing two things at once—evaluating vehicles and keeping track of their children. The moment the kids get bored or start running around, the parents' focus splits, and the conversation gets harder.

Acknowledge the kids briefly and naturally. Not in a way that feels like a sales technique—"Oh, what a great family!" is cringeworthy and everyone knows it. Just a normal human acknowledgment. "How old are they?" or a simple smile and hello to the kids goes a long way.

If there's a waiting area or a place where kids can sit, mention it. You're not moving the kids out of the way for your benefit. You're offering the parents an option that makes the conversation easier for them.

Don't let the kids be the reason the conversation ends early. A little awareness of the family dynamic goes a long way toward keeping everyone comfortable long enough to have a real conversation.

Multiple Adults

Sometimes it's more than two—a person bringing a parent, a couple with a friend who knows cars, siblings shopping together. The dynamics vary, but the principle stays the same: acknowledge everyone, identify who's making the decision, and don't let anyone feel irrelevant.

The person who seems like a secondary figure may be the most important one in the room. They may be the one whose opinion the buyer trusts most. Treat everyone like they matter—because in these situations, they usually do.

"The Rule: Every person who got out of that car has a role in the decision. Find out what it is before you decide who deserves your attention."

APPROACHING THE CUSTOMER WHO WON'T MAKE EYE CONTACT

EVERY LOT HAS THEM. The customer who pulls in, gets out, and keeps their eyes on the vehicles—the ground, their phone, anywhere but you. You start across the lot, and they're already looking away. You get close, and they still haven't looked up.

New salespeople panic at this. They read it as hostility, or disinterest, or a signal that this person doesn't want to be helped.

Most of the time, it's none of those things.

What It Usually Means

Avoiding eye contact is one of the most common ways people manage social discomfort. On a car lot, where customers already feel a degree of pressure before they arrive, it's even more common.

The customer who won't make eye contact is usually telling you one of three things.

I'm nervous about this interaction, and I'm not ready for it yet. Give me a minute.

I've had bad experiences before, and I'm keeping my guard up until I know what this is going to be like.

I'm already focused on something specific, and I'm in my own head about it.

None of those things means they don't want to buy a car. They mean they need the approach to be softer, slower, and less demanding than the standard greeting.

What Not to Do

Don't try to force eye contact. Moving around the vehicle to get in front of them, positioning yourself so they have to look at you, or calling out to them from across the lot to make them turn around—all of that escalates the discomfort. You're trying to solve the problem by doing the thing that created it.

Don't interpret the lack of eye contact as a rejection and retreat. Walking away entirely, or giving up on the approach because they seem closed off, means you've let their discomfort end a conversation that hadn't started yet.

And don't over-compensate with enthusiasm. Ramping up your energy to try to break through their reserve almost always makes it worse. The customer who's already guarded doesn't respond well to a salesperson who comes at them harder.

What Works

Come in low-key. Even lower than your standard approach.

Approach at a relaxed pace, stop at a comfortable distance, and deliver a greeting that asks absolutely nothing of them. No question. No invitation to talk. Just an acknowledgment.

"Hey—I'm Bruce. Take your time. I'll be around if you need anything."

Then don't stand there waiting for a response. Step back, or move to a position nearby that doesn't feel like surveillance. You've made contact, you've given them your name, you've made clear you're available—now give them room to breathe.

What you're doing is lowering the stakes of the interaction. You're showing them that talking to you doesn't cost anything, that you're not going to lock them into a conversation, that they're in control of when and whether the next moment happens.

That's what the avoidant customer needs to hear before they'll look up.

The Follow-Up

Give them a few minutes. Then come back—but come back with something practical, not another open-ended offer to help.

"That one you're looking at—did you want to see the inside? I can grab the keys."

A specific, low-demand offer connected to what they're already doing is much easier for an avoidant customer to respond to than a general "Do you have any questions?" It gives them a concrete yes or no rather than requiring them to volunteer information or initiate a conversation.

Often, that's the moment the wall comes down. Not all the way. But enough.

The customer who wouldn't look at you ten minutes ago is now talking about the vehicle in front of them. That's not magic—that's patience, a light approach, and a follow-up that met them where they were.

When It's Actually Hostility

Occasionally, the lack of eye contact really is intentional. The customer is signaling—as clearly as they can without saying it—that they don't want the interaction.

You'll know this is the case when the other signals are there too: turned body, short clipped responses if they respond at all, deliberate movement away from you when you approach.

In that case, respect it. Give the greeting, step back, and stay available without hovering. If they want help, they know you're there. If they don't, pushing won't change that—and it might cost you the deal entirely.

Not every customer is ready for the conversation on your timeline. The ones who aren't sometimes come around when they feel like the choice is theirs.

"The Rule: The customer who won't make eye contact isn't rejecting you. They're managing discomfort. Lower the stakes of the interaction and give them room to come to you."

CHAPTER 9

THE SIT-IN-THE-CAR CUSTOMER

THEY PULL IN, THEY park, and they don't get out.

You're watching from inside. A minute goes by. Two minutes. They're still in there. Maybe they're on the phone. Maybe they're finishing a conversation. Maybe they're sitting with their hands on the wheel, not quite ready to do this yet.

What do you do?

Most salespeople either wait too long or move too fast. Both create problems. Understanding what's happening in that car—and what the right response is—makes this a solvable situation instead of an awkward one.

Why They're Still in the Car

There are a few common reasons a customer sits in their vehicle after pulling in, and almost none of them are bad signs.

Finishing something. A call, a text, a thought. They're just wrapping up before they shift into this. Give them the moment. Don't be the person who walks out and makes them feel rushed before they've even opened the door.

Building up to it. Some customers need a beat before they walk onto a lot. They know this is going to involve a salesperson and are mentally preparing for it. Sitting in the car is the deep breath before the door opens.

Observing first. They're watching the lot, watching the staff, getting a feel for the place before they commit to getting out. They're gathering information. That's not hesitation—that's due diligence.

Confirming the decision. They're double-checking something on their phone—a price they researched, a model number, a picture of the vehicle they came to look at. They know what they want. They just want to make sure they have the details straight before they go in.

In most of these cases, they're going to get out. They just need a minute.

The Timing

Two to three minutes is a reasonable window. Before that, you're going to them before they're ready. After that, you risk them feeling as if they could have been standing on your lot for five minutes without anyone noticing.

If they're visibly on the phone, give them until they're done. Walking out to a customer who's mid-call forces them to either end the call or wave you off—neither of which starts things on the right foot.

If they're just sitting there, two minutes is about right. Then go.

The Approach

Walk out at your normal pace. Don't hover near the door waiting for them to get out—that's more pressure, not less. Go to them naturally, the way you'd walk toward anyone on the lot.

If they're still in the car when you arrive, position yourself a comfortable distance from the driver's door—not right up against it—and give a relaxed wave or a friendly nod as they notice you. Let them open the door themselves. Don't reach for the handle.

When they get out, introduce yourself simply.

"Hey—I'm Bruce. Take your time looking around. I'll be right here if you need anything."

No comment about how long they've been sitting there. No "I was wondering if you were coming in." No joke about the weather or the wait. Just a normal greeting as if they'd walked up like anyone else.

When They're Still Not Getting Out

Sometimes you go out, and they're still in the car. They see you coming, but they don't move.

In that case, a light wave from a respectful distance is enough. You're not going to stand at their window. You're letting them know you've seen them and you're available. Then step back toward the front of the lot or into a position where you're visible but not looming.

Give them another minute or two. If they're still in the car, they may not be sure about getting out at all—they may be deciding whether this is the right dealership, the right day, the right decision. That's their process. You can't rush it from the outside.

Some of them will come out when they're ready. Some won't. Either way, hovering next to their car won't change the outcome.

FROM THE FLOOR

One afternoon, a customer pulled into the lot in a taxi. That caught my attention—most people drive themselves in. This one stepped out and walked directly toward a specific vehicle, as if he already knew exactly what he was looking for.

I didn't rush. I stood up, walked out at a normal pace, and gave him a small wave as I crossed the lot. When I reached him, I introduced myself and told him I'd be glad to help if he had any questions.

He told me he'd just gotten off a flight and came straight from the airport. His vehicle was destroyed in a parking lot fire while he was traveling. He'd seen one of our ads and came directly to us. He knew which vehicle he wanted. He just needed to drive it and confirm it.

We took a short test drive. Came back. He asked how to make out the check.

Start to finish, maybe forty-five minutes. The deal was easy because the approach was right. No pressure, no assumptions, no rushing. Just a professional greeting and a willingness to follow the customer's lead.

Not every customer comes in ready to buy. But every customer deserves that same professional opening. You never know which one will be the taxi customer—the one who's already decided and just needs someone not to get in their way.

That customer didn't sit in a car—he arrived in someone else's. But the principle is the same. You don't know what someone's situation is until you give them a chance to tell you. A patient, professional approach is what makes that possible.

The sit-in-the-car customer isn't a problem to solve. They're a person deciding their own pace. Give them the space to make it.

"The Rule: When the customer is still in the car, the right move is patience and a calm approach—not pressure. They'll get out when they're ready. Your job is to make sure it's worth it when they do."

CHAPTER 10

THE DRIVE-BY: WHEN THEY'RE NOT GETTING OUT

I T HAPPENS MORE THAN you'd think. A car pulls onto the lot, does a slow loop, and pulls back out. Or it comes through the entrance, slows near a row of vehicles, then keeps going.

The drive-by.

Most salespeople watch it happen and write it off. They were just looking. Didn't want to stop. Not serious.

Sometimes that's true. But not always—and the difference matters.

Why People Drive By

The slow drive-through is rarely random. People do it for reasons, and those reasons tell you something about where they are in the buying process.

They're scoping before they commit. They want to know what the lot looks like, what kind of inventory you have, what the general feel of the place is—before they decide whether getting out is worth it. This is reconnaissance. If the lot passes the test, they may come back. Maybe today. Maybe next week.

They spotted something specific. They drove past a vehicle that caught their eye and slowed to look at it. They may not have been planning to stop, but something on your lot gave them a reason to reconsider.

They're nervous about stopping. Pulling onto the lot and getting out feels like a commitment. Driving through feels less like one. They can tell themselves they were just passing by. It's a lower-stakes version of being there.

They're comparing lots. They're conducting a first-pass survey of multiple dealerships before deciding where to spend their time. They're not your customer yet—but they could be.

None of these people is a bad prospect. Some of them are better prospects than they look.

What You Can Do

If the vehicle is moving and hasn't stopped, your options are limited. You're not going to flag it down. You're not going to step into the path of a moving car. And you're not going to stand in the lot making big gestures hoping they'll notice you.

What you can do is be visible. Stand near the front of the lot or at the entrance, in a way that conveys presence without aggression. A natural, relaxed stance—not hovering, not pacing—that says, "Someone is here, and it's a professional operation."

If the car slows near another vehicle or the window comes down, that's your signal. Walk toward them calmly. Don't run. Don't rush.

"Hey—how's it going? Looking for anything specific?"

Keep it light. You're not trying to close them from the lot entrance. You're trying to create a moment that makes them feel like stopping is a reasonable idea.

If They Stop Briefly

Sometimes the drive-by turns into a brief stop. The car parks for a minute, they look at something, and you can see they're not fully committed to getting out.

This is the moment to approach—but carefully: a slow walk, a friendly wave from a distance. Not bearing down on them before they've had a chance to decide whether they're staying.

If they get out, great—treat it like any other approach. If they don't, a simple wave and a "Feel free to look around—I'll be out here if you need anything" gives them something without demanding a response.

You've acknowledged them. You've made yourself available. You haven't made getting out of the car feel like the beginning of a high-pressure sales experience.

That alone might be enough to bring them back.

The Follow-Up

If they leave without stopping, there's nothing to follow up on directly. You don't have a name. You don't have contact information. What you have is the knowledge that someone came through your lot and looked.

What you can control is what happens if they come back. And the customers who do a drive-by first often do come back—because the lot passed the visual test, because they saw something that stayed with them. After all, the professional presence they noticed gave them enough confidence actually to stop next time.

Be the kind of lot—be the kind of salesperson—that makes the second visit feel worth the first stop. That's the long game on the drive-by, and it's the only game available.

What the Drive-By Tells You About Your Lot

A lot of drive-bys with no follow-through is also information. It may mean the lot looks uninviting from the road. It may mean vehicles are positioned in a way that doesn't show them well. It may mean customers are driving through and not seeing anything that makes them want to stop.

That's a management conversation, not a sales conversation. But it's worth paying attention to. The approach starts before a customer ever gets out of the car—and for drive-by customers, before they even pull in.

"The Rule: The drive-by isn't a lost customer. It's a customer at an earlier stage of the decision-making process. Be visible, be professional, and be the reason they come back."

CHAPTER 11

RECOVERING A BAD APPROACH

I T'S GOING TO HAPPEN. Maybe it already has.

You walked out too fast. You said the wrong thing. You approached a couple and talked exclusively to one of them. You asked a question that put the customer on the spot, and now they're giving you one-word answers and looking for an exit.

The approach went sideways. The question is what you do next.

Most salespeople do one of two things at this point. They push harder, trying to power through the awkwardness with enthusiasm and more questions. Or they give up, retreat, and mentally write the customer off.

Neither works. There's a third option, and it's the one that actually gives you a chance to recover the deal.

First: Recognize It

Recovery starts with recognizing that something went wrong. That sounds obvious, but many salespeople miss it. They're in their own head—thinking about what to say next, running through their process—and they don't notice that the customer in front of them has closed off.

The signals are clear once you know what to look for. Short answers. Avoided eye contact. Physical distance—they've taken a step back, or turned slightly away. Responses that end the topic rather than continuing it. A general flatness where there should be some kind of energy.

When you see those signals, stop. Not literally—you don't freeze mid-sentence. But mentally, stop pushing forward and start adjusting.

What Not to Do

Don't apologize dramatically. "I'm sorry, I feel like I came on too strong—let me start over." This puts the awkwardness front and center and makes the customer feel like they need to respond to your apology on top of everything else. It's well-intentioned, and it usually makes things worse.

Don't ramp up your energy to try to change the mood. A customer who's already closed off doesn't reopen because you got more enthusiastic. That's more of what already didn't work.

Don't disappear entirely. Retreating to the building and leaving the customer alone on the lot is the other extreme. You've now made them feel like they were difficult, or like you gave up on them. Neither is a good setup for what comes next.

The Reset

The reset is simple, and it works almost every time.

Pull back. Physically and conversationally. Create a little space—step back a foot or two, lower your energy, slow the pace of what you're saying.

Then shift to something with no pressure. Not another question about what they're looking for or their budget. Something practical and specific about what they're already looking at.

"That one's actually just come in—haven't even had a chance to put a sticker on it yet."

"If you want to look inside, I can grab the keys."

"Take your time—I'll be right over here if anything comes up."

You're not trying to restart the conversation from the beginning. You're lowering the temperature and giving the customer a way to re-engage on their own terms. A specific, low-demand comment about the vehicle they're standing next to is usually enough to shift the dynamic.

It removes the pressure from the interaction and replaces it with something practical. They can respond to that or not. Either way, you've stepped back from whatever was creating the problem.

Give Them Space, Then Come Back

After the reset, step away. Not far—just enough. Fifteen to twenty feet. Stay visible. Be available without hovering.

Give them three to five minutes to breathe. Then come back with something specific and concrete—a question about the vehicle they've been looking at, an offer to open it up, a piece of relevant information.

"That one has the towing package—I don't know if that matters to you, but it's hard to find on a used one at this price."

You're coming back in through a different door. Not the door that didn't work. A door that's about information they might actually find useful, with no ask attached.

Customers who were closed off five minutes ago open back up more often than you'd expect when they've had a chance to decompress, and the salesperson comes back differently.

When It's Not Recoverable

Sometimes the approach went badly enough that the customer was done. They've already made up their mind. They're going through the motions of looking at one or two more things before they leave.

You'll know. The signals are unmistakable—they're moving toward the exit, they're not engaging with vehicles anymore, they're looking at you as an obstacle rather than a resource.

In that case, end with dignity. "Hey—I appreciate you coming in. If anything comes up later, here's my card."

No guilt trip. No last-ditch pitch. A clean, professional close to an interaction that didn't go as you'd hoped.

Some of those customers come back. Not most of them. But some. And the ones who do remember how they were treated at the end, not just at the beginning.

What a Bad Approach Teaches You

Every bad approach is information. If you're paying attention, it tells you something specific about what went wrong—where the customer closed off, what triggered it, what you might do differently next time.

The salespeople who consistently improve their approach are the ones who treat every interaction, including the failed ones, as opportunities to learn—not to obsess over or beat themselves up about—but to just notice, adjust, and carry that adjustment into the next one.

You're going to have bad approaches. The goal isn't to eliminate them. The goal is to recover from them when they happen and to make them less frequent over time.

"The Rule: A bad approach isn't the end of the deal. It's information. Pull back, lower the pressure, and find a different door. Some of them open."

CHAPTER 12

BUILDING AN APPROACH THAT FITS YOU

EVERYTHING IN THIS BOOK is a framework, not a formula. The principles are real—distance, pace, opening language, and reading the customer before you arrive—but none of it is a script you execute the same way every time. The approach that works is the one that becomes yours.

That takes time and attention. Here's how to build it.

Start with What You Already Do Well

Most salespeople have at least one natural strength in the approach, even if they haven't identified it yet.

Some people are genuinely warm. Customers feel it the moment they arrive. If that's you, that's your foundation. Build everything else around it.

Some people are calm under pressure. They don't get rattled when a customer is cold or short. They can absorb the resistance and keep going without taking it personally. That's a significant advantage on the lot. Use it.

Some people are naturally good readers. They pick up on cues—body language, pace, tone—faster than most. They know before they arrive whether the customer is open or guarded. That instinct is worth more than most training can teach.

Figure out what you already bring. Then build the rest of the approach around that strength rather than trying to replace it with a technique that doesn't fit who you are.

Identify What's Getting in the Way

With the same honesty, identify what's not working.

Do you approach too fast? Do you talk too much in the first thirty seconds? Do you default to questions that put customers on the spot? Do you ignore the passenger? Do you give up too easily when the first response is cool?

You probably know the answer. Most salespeople do. The problem isn't awareness—it's that old habits are comfortable, and changing them requires deliberate attention on every single approach until the new behavior replaces the old one.

Pick one thing. Not five things—one. Fix that. Then pick the next one.

Trying to overhaul your entire approach at once is how nothing gets better. Fixing one specific habit at a time is how salespeople actually improve.

Practice Outside the Lot

The approach is a set of social skills that improve with practice in any context—not just on the lot.

Pay attention to how you enter conversations in your daily life. When you walk into a room and don't know everyone there, what do you do? When you approach a stranger to ask for directions, how do you open? When you run into an acquaintance you don't know well, how do those first 30 seconds go?

These are all versions of the same skill. The awareness you build in those moments transfers directly to the lot.

You can also practice specific elements. Your opening line, in front of a mirror or with a colleague. The pace of your walk across a room. How do you position yourself relative to someone when you stop to talk? None of it is complicated, but all of it benefits from conscious repetition before the stakes are real.

Pay Attention to What Works

After every approach that goes well—where the customer relaxes, where the conversation opens up, where you feel the dynamic shift in your favor—ask yourself what you did.

Not in a general way. Specifically. What was the pace like? What did you say first? Where did you stand? How long did you wait before you approached?

When you can identify specifically what worked, you can repeat it deliberately. That's how a consistent approach gets built—not from training materials, but from your own experience, examined carefully.

Do the same after approaches that don't go well. Not to beat yourself up. To extract the lesson and carry it forward.

Let It Evolve

The approach you use in your first year won't be the same as the one you use in your fifth. It shouldn't be. You're going to learn things about customers, about yourself, about what works in your specific market and at your specific dealership that will change how you do this.

Stay open to that. The salespeople who stop learning are the ones who peaked early. The ones who keep getting better are the ones who treat every day on the lot as more information about how to do this well.

Build an approach that fits who you are right now. Then keep building it.

FROM THE FLOOR

I had a colleague who couldn't get any traction with a woman at the used-car lot. She kept saying she was just looking. He couldn't figure out what was off—he'd done everything right as far as he could tell. He came and got me.

I went out, introduced myself, and asked how I could help her.

She said: "God, thank you. I really want to buy this car. But that other guy looks exactly like my ex-husband, and I cannot stand the sight of him."

Nothing to do with the car. Nothing to do with the approach. She knew exactly what she wanted—she just needed a different person in front of her before she would let the conversation happen. We tested the vehicle, worked out fair numbers, and she drove home happy.

Don't take "I'm just looking" personally. Don't take it as a verdict. Take it as information—something needs to be adjusted. Sometimes that's your approach. Sometimes it's giving more space. And occasionally it's a different person entirely. All of those are workable. None of them is the end of the deal.

That story belongs in this chapter because it makes the point better than anything else can. You can do everything right and still be the wrong fit for a particular customer in a particular moment. That's not a failure of your approach—it's the reality of working with people.

Build an approach that works for most customers most of the time. And stay flexible enough to recognize when the situation calls for something different.

"The Rule: The best approach is the one that's genuinely yours. Build it from your strengths, fix what gets in the way, and keep refining it for as long as you're in this business."

CHAPTER 13

THE APPROACH CHECKLIST

THIS IS THE SHORT version. Everything in this book is distilled into a checklist you can run through in the few seconds between spotting a customer and walking out the door.

It's not a script. It's a set of reminders—the things that are easy to forget when you're in motion, when you're tired, when the lot is busy, or when you've been having a slow day, and you're more eager than you should be.

Run it before every approach. Especially on the days when you think you don't need to.

Before You Walk Out

Watch first. Take ten to fifteen seconds before you move. Where did they go? Who got out of the car? What are they looking at? What does their body language tell you about their comfort level?

Slow down. If you feel urgency—if your instinct is to get out there fast—that's the signal to slow your pace deliberately. Urgency in the salesperson's tone comes across as pressure to the customer.

Check yourself. Are you in the right headspace? A distracted or frustrated salesperson carries that energy onto the lot, and customers feel it. Take a breath. Be present.

The Walk

Normal pace. Not slow, not fast. The pace of someone going to say hello to a person they're glad to see.

Open posture. Shoulders back, hands visible and relaxed. Not crossed, not in pockets, not holding anything that creates a barrier.

No urgency in the body. If your walk looks like you're racing to claim the customer before someone else does, that's exactly how it reads.

The Arrival

Distance. Stop at six to eight feet. Close enough to be clearly engaged, but far enough not to be in their space.

Angle. Slightly off-center rather than squarely face-to-face. Side-by-side feels like collaboration. Face-to-face feels like confrontation.

Eye contact. Natural, not intense. A genuine acknowledgment, not a stare.

Acknowledge everyone. If there's more than one person, make eye contact with all of them before you finish the greeting.

The Opening

Give your name. Simple. "Hey—I'm Bruce." They know who they're talking to, and giving a name is an act of openness.

Ask nothing. The opening line doesn't ask for information, commitment, or a decision. It offers something—a welcome, availability, permission to take their time.

Keep it short. Two sentences at most. The opening is not the place for information or enthusiasm. It's the place for a low-pressure beginning.

Match your tone to your words. A warm greeting delivered in a flat voice is just a script. Mean it.

After the Opening

Read the response. Did they engage or pull back? Are they making eye contact or avoiding it? Did they ask a question or give a one-word answer?

Follow their lead. If they engage, step into the conversation. If they pull back, step back and give them space.

Stay available. Whether they engage immediately or need time, stay in a position where they can find you when they're ready—not hovering. Not gone. Available.

Throughout the Conversation

Listen more than you talk. Customers tell you what they need. You have to be quiet long enough to hear it.

Watch the signals. Are they getting more comfortable or less? Are they moving toward vehicles or away from them? Are their responses getting longer or shorter?

Adjust continuously. The approach doesn't end when you say hello. You're reading and adjusting throughout the entire interaction.

The Reminder

Every customer on that lot is making a significant decision. Most of them came in hoping it would go better than they expected. Your job is to be the reason it does.

That starts with the approach. Get it right, and everything that follows has a chance.

"The Rule: The checklist isn't a substitute for skill—it's a tool for keeping your skill sharp. Run it every time. The days you think you don't need it are usually the days you need it most."

Conclusion

The approach is the smallest moment in the sales process and one of the most consequential.

It takes maybe thirty seconds. In those thirty seconds, the customer decides whether they're comfortable or guarded, whether they're going to talk to you or manage you, whether this is going to be the experience they feared or something better than they expected.

You don't get a second chance at it. But you get a new one with every customer who pulls onto the lot.

What this book aims to give you is a clear picture of what's actually happening in that moment—from both sides —and of what the customer is thinking before you reach them, and what your pace, distance, and posture communicate before you open your mouth. What words open a conversation, and what words shut one down? How to handle the customer who won't make eye contact, the couple where one person is invisible, the person still sitting in their car, the one who drives through and keeps going.

None of it is complicated. None of it requires a special personality or a natural gift for sales. What it requires is attention—to the customer in front of you, to the signals they're sending, and to the habits you've developed that may be working against you without your knowing it.

The salespeople who are consistently good at the approach have one thing in common: they treat it like a skill. Not a formality, not a hurdle to clear on the way to the real conversation, but a skill—something to be developed, refined, and paid attention to every single time.

That's what separates good salespeople from great ones. Not talent. Not luck. Not a better territory or a better inventory. The willingness to treat the smallest moment in the process as something worth getting right.

Go get it right.

Tips for the Sales Manager

The approach problems on your lot are not individual. There are cultural problems. And culture is your responsibility.

If your salespeople are sprinting to cars, it's because they feel like they have to. If they're ignoring passengers, it's because no one has ever held them accountable. If they're opening with questions that close down the conversation, it's because those habits formed without correction and hardened over time.

You can't fix those things from your desk. Here's where to start.

Watch the Approach

Actually watch it. Not from across the showroom floor through the glass—close enough to see what's happening. How fast are your people walking out? Where are they stopping? What's the customer's body language when the salesperson arrives?

You'll see things you didn't know were happening. Most managers are surprised the first time they actually observe the approach with intention. The sprint. The immediate question. The focus is entirely on the driver, while the passenger stands there. These habits are invisible to the people who have them. They won't be invisible to you.

Debrief Every Lost Customer

"They were just looking" is not a debrief. It's a conclusion without an analysis.

Ask your salespeople specific questions about what happened. When did the customer arrive? How long before they were approached? What was the opening line? What did the customer say? When did the conversation end, and what was happening right before it did?

You're not interrogating them. You're teaching them to think about what happened rather than just accepting the outcome. That habit of analysis is how salespeople improve. Most of them won't develop it on their own. You have to build it into the culture.

Set Clear Expectations

Your salespeople should know exactly what a professional approach looks like on your lot. Not in general terms—specifically. What's the expected timing from when a customer arrives to when they're greeted? What's the standard for acknowledging everyone at the party? Which opening lines represent your dealership well, and which don't?

If those expectations aren't explicit, your salespeople are making them up. And they're making them up based on what's comfortable for them, not what's effective for the customer.

Write it down. Talk about it in your morning meetings. Reference it when you debrief. Make the standard visible and consistent.

Role-Play It

I know. Nobody likes role-play. Do it anyway.

The approach is a physical skill—pace, distance, posture, and opening line. You can talk about it all day, but talking about it doesn't build the muscle memory. Practice does.

Run it in your morning meeting. Have a salesperson approach you as if you're a customer. Give them real-time feedback on pace, distance, and the opening. Then switch. Show them what it should look like. Let them see the difference.

Five minutes of practice before the lot opens is worth more than an hour of training material.

Recognize What's Working

When you see a salesperson nail the approach—calm pace, right distance, clean opening, genuine acknowledgment of everyone in the party—say something. Not a performance review comment. A real, specific observation in the moment.

"I watched that approach. You gave them space, you introduced yourself to both of them, and you didn't ask for anything in the first thirty seconds. That's exactly what it should look like."

Specific positive feedback on a specific behavior is the fastest way to reinforce it. Your salespeople will remember exactly what you recognized, and they'll do it again.

The Standard Is Yours to Set

The approach culture on your lot is a direct reflection of what you tolerate and what you reward. If you tolerate the sprint, you get the sprint. If you reward the patient with a professional approach, you get that instead.

It doesn't change overnight. But it changes. And it starts with you deciding that the approach is something worth paying attention to.

APPENDIX

The Rules

Every chapter in this book ends with The Rule—the single most important principle from that chapter, stated plainly. Collected here for quick reference.

Introduction: The sale doesn't start when the customer says yes. It starts the moment they see you coming.

Chapter 1: A bad approach doesn't just cost you a greeting. It costs you the conversation—and everything that conversation could have led to.

Chapter 2: Customers decide how this is going to feel before you open your mouth. The approach is your only chance to change the answer they've already begun to form.

Chapter 3: The distance you keep when you arrive tells the customer whether you're coming to help them or coming at them. Get it right before you say hello.

Chapter 4: Read before you walk. The few seconds between them pulling in and you going out are the only free information you'll get about who they are and what they need.

Chapter 5: Your opening line has one job: make the next moment possible. Keep it simple, keep it genuine, and ask nothing of the customer before they're ready to give it.

Chapter 6: With a solo buyer, your presence is concentrated. Give them a little more space, a little more time, and a door they can walk through when they're ready.

Chapter 7: Every person who got out of that car has a role in the decision. Find out what it is before you decide who deserves your attention.

Chapter 8: The customer who won't make eye contact isn't rejecting you. They're managing discomfort. Lower the stakes of the interaction and give them room to come to you.

Chapter 9: When the customer is still in the car, the right move is patience and a calm approach—not pressure. They'll get out when they're ready. Your job is to make sure it's worth it when they do.

Chapter 10: The drive-by isn't a lost customer. It's a customer in an earlier stage of the decision. Be visible, be professional, and be the reason they come back.

Chapter 11: A bad approach isn't the end of the deal. It's information. Pull back, lower the pressure, and find a different door. Some of them open.

Chapter 12: The best approach is the one that's genuinely yours. Build it from your strengths, fix what gets in the way, and keep refining it for as long as you're in this business.

Chapter 13: The checklist isn't a substitute for skill—it's a tool for keeping your skill sharp. Run it every time. The days you think you don't need it are usually the days you need it most.

Also Available

from Bedrock Heritage Publishing

FLAGSHIP

The Complete Car Sales Survival Guide

The No-BS Playbook for New Automotive Salespeople

Book 1 — The Meet and Greet Playbook

How to Make Powerful First Impressions with Customers, Clients, and Guests

Book 2 — The First 60 Seconds in Car Sales

A Proven Meet and Greet System to Build Trust and Start More Conversations

Book 3 — How to Handle "I'm Just Looking" in Car Sales

A Simple System to Turn Brush-Offs into Productive Conversations

Book 4 — Body Language in Car Sales

How Posture, Eye Contact, and Presence Build Customer Trust

Book 5 — Greeting Customers on the Lot

How to Approach Buyers Without Pressure

Book 6 — The Ten-Second Rule in Car Sales

Why First Impressions Determine Whether Customers Stay or Leave

Book 7 — The Car Sales Conversation Starter Guide

How to Begin Natural Conversations That Lead to Sales

Book 8 — Car Sales Confidence for New Salespeople

How to Approach Customers Without Fear or Hesitation

Book 9 — Common Car Sales Greeting Mistakes

What Drives Customers Away in the First Minute

Book 10 — The First Five Minutes With a Car Buyer

How to Transition from Greeting to Conversation and Move Toward the Sale

WORK WITH BRUCE

If you're interested in one-on-one coaching, sales team training, or dealership consulting, Bruce works with individuals and organizations through Life Guidance Consulting.

For inquiries:

www.lifeguidanceconsulting.com

bruce@lifeguidanceconsulting.com

For publishing inquiries or bulk orders:

www.bedrockheritagepublishing.com

info@bedrockheritagepublishing.com

About the Author

Bruce Huddleston spent thirty-five years in the automotive industry, working every level of the business from showroom floor salesperson to finance manager, sales manager, used car manager, and general manager. His career included new-car franchise dealerships, independent used-car operations, and a decade in buy-here, pay-here—giving him a breadth of experience that few in the industry can match.

He began as a high school dropout who needed a job and ended up discovering a profession. He ended as a veteran who had trained hundreds of salespeople, managed multiple departments, and built a reputation for straight talk in an industry that doesn't always reward it.

Since retiring, Bruce has opened a life coaching practice, assists his wife with her mental health therapy practice, and operates Bedrock Heritage Publishing, a division of Life Guidance Consulting LLC, where he writes practical guides for sales professionals across multiple industries.

The Complete Car Sales Survival Guide is his flagship work. The Car Sales Survival Guide Series—a collection of focused training guides on specific sales skills—is built on the same foundation of real experience, honest insight, and zero tolerance for the kind of nonsense that gives sales a bad name.

He lives in Tyler, Texas.

A Quick Favor

If *Greeting Customers on the Lot* helped you — if it changed how you walk onto a lot, how you read a customer, or how you think about what your body is saying before you open your mouth — I'd be grateful if you'd take two minutes to leave a review wherever you bought it.

Reviews matter more than most people realize. They help other salespeople find books that can actually make a difference in their work. And honest feedback helps me keep writing things worth reading. You can simply scan the QR code below.

https://www.amazon.com/review/create-review/?asin=1972179136

www.bedrockheritagepublishing.com

Thank you for spending time with this book. Now go to work.
— Bruce Huddleston